IF EVER YOU GO
TO DUBLIN TOWN

IF EVER YOU GO
TO DUBLIN TOWN

PHOTOGRAPHS
ELINOR WILTSHIRE

TEXT
ORLA FITZPATRICK

NATIONAL LIBRARY OF IRELAND
WOMEN'S HISTORY PROJECT

Published by the Women's History Project and the National Library of Ireland, 1999

© National Library of Ireland, 1999

Reprinted 2002

British Library Cataloguing in Publication information available.

ISBN 0907328180

Design and typesetting by Dunbar Design
Printed by Betaprint

These photographs, mainly of Dublin and its people, were taken over a period of about fifteen years. They began with the acquisition around 1955 of a Rolleiflex camera. Holding it at waist level, a scene could be viewed by looking down at a 6x6cm ground-glass screen. This meant that people were often unaware that pictures were being taken. It is also very good for framing buildings and composing scenes.

It was a pleasure to go round Dublin in those days, recording with affection various features of human and historic interest, some at the suggestion of Patrick Kavanagh or Desmond Guinness.

During most of this period my husband, Reggie Wiltshire, and I operated The Green Studio in Stephen's Green. Although these pictures were separate from commercial activities, the studio provided the essential infrastructure for processing and printing, and I am grateful for the contribution made by members of our team.

Reggie's death in 1968 led to the sale of the business, and to the conclusion of this series of photographs. For over a quarter-century I kept the negatives and albums of prints, unused, until happily they were acquired by the National Library of Ireland for the National Photographic Archive.

18 AUGUST 1999
ELINOR WILTSHIRE
LONDON

IF EVER YOU GO
TO DUBLIN TOWN

If ever you go to Dublin town
In a hundred years or so
Inquire for me in Baggot Street
And what I was like to know.
O he was a queer one,
Fol dol the di do,
He was a queer one
I tell you.

My great-grandmother knew him well,
He asked her to come and call
On him in his flat and she giggled at the thought
Of a young girl's lovely fall.
O he was dangerous,
Fol dol the di do,
He was dangerous
I tell you.

On Pembroke Road look out for my ghost,
Dishevelled with shoes untied,
Playing through the railings with little children
Whose children have long since died.
O he was a nice man,
Fol dol the di do,
He was a nice man
I tell you.

Go into a pub and listen well
If my voice still echoes there,
Ask the men what their grandsires thought
And tell them to answer fair.
O he was eccentric,
Fol dol the di do,
He was eccentric
I tell you.

He had the knack of making men feel
As small as they really were
Which meant as great as God had made them
But as males they disliked his air.
O he was a proud one,
Fol dol the di do,
He was a proud one
I tell you.

If ever you go to Dublin town
In a hundred years or so
Sniff for my personality,
Is it Vanity's vapour now?
O he was a vain one,
Fol dol the di do,
He was a vain one
I tell you.

I saw his name with a hundred others
In a book in the library,
It said he had never fully achieved
His potentiality.
O he was slothful,
Fol dol the di do,
He was slothful
I tell you.

He knew that posterity has no use
For anything but the soul,
The lines that speak the passionate heart,
The spirit that lives alone.
O he was a lone one,
Fol dol the di do
Yet he lived happily
I tell you.

PATRICK KAVANAGH

PREFACE

This publication is one of the outcomes of a successful collaboration between the National Library's Photographic Archive, established in 1998, and the Women's History Project, which began work in 1997.

The Archive, located in Meeting House Square, in Dublin's Temple Bar area, now houses the entire photographic collections of the National Library of Ireland comprising approximately 300,000 photographs, the vast majority of which are Irish. Subject matter ranges from topographical views to studio portraits, and from political events to early tourist photographs.[1]

A joint venture between the Library and the Women's History Project enabled the post of researcher to be created in 1998, with support from the Heritage Council, for the purpose of researching and cataloguing the Wiltshire Collection of photographs which had been acquired by the Library in 1994. Extensive work has since been carried out on the collection of 1,000 negatives and 300 prints. Locations were identified, titles assigned and the entire collection was catalogued onto the National Library's computer system for ease of access. A selection of images from the collection went on exhibition at the Archive in July 1999 and this publication marks the completion of the next phase of the project. The entire collection can be viewed at the Photographic Archive.

Work on the Wiltshire collection fits in well with the aims of the Women's History Project which are to survey, list and publish documents relating to the history of women in Ireland. The Project is managed by a committee appointed by the Women's History Association of Ireland, and is made up of archivists, librarians and history teachers, as well as academic historians. The work completed by the Project to date has already opened up new areas of study allowing for a greater understanding of the diverse experiences of women in Irish history.[2]

This representative sample of Elinor Wiltshire's work permanently records her unique vision of Dublin town at a particular time, yet the themes remain relevant to the city of today.

MARIA LUDDY
DIRECTOR
WOMEN'S HISTORY PROJECT

BRENDAN O'DONOGHUE
DIRECTOR
NATIONAL LIBRARY OF IRELAND

1   Sarah Rouse, *Into the Light, an Illustrated Guide to the Photographic Collections in the National Library of Ireland,* NLI, 1998

2   Publications of the Women's History Project include:

Jean Agnew and Maria Luddy (eds.) *The Drennan-McTier Letters, 1776–1819,* 3 volumes (The Women's History Project/Irish Manuscripts Commission: Dublin, 1998/1999).

A Directory of Sources for Women's History in Ireland, available on CD-ROM, which incorporates the results of a survey of over three hundred private and public repositories in the Republic of Ireland and Northern Ireland.

A calendar of the papers of the Ulster Unionist Women's Council, 1911–1942, edited by Diane Urquhart.

INTRODUCTION

The images featured in this book were created by Limerick-born Elinor Wiltshire who, together with her husband, Reginald – himself an accomplished photographer – established the Green Studios at St. Stephen's Green, Dublin in the 1950s. The studios executed high-quality commercial work for many years but it is with Elinor's own photographs, taken on weekends between 1950 and 1970 that this

book is concerned. Her photographs mainly show Dublin street scenes and chronicle the dramatic changes taking place in the city at the time. Elinor's love of Dublin and it's people provided the inspiration for these vibrant and moving portraits of city life. In 1954, she visited travellers at their campsites in Galway and Cork and these photographs show a traditional way of life that was soon to decline. These subjects, coupled with her photographs of literary figures, met through her friendship with Patrick Kavanagh, make this collection an invaluable record of Irish life during this period. The attraction of the collection transcends mere nostalgia for times past as Elinor's images show real photographic talent and personal vision. The near perfect composition in many of the images reveals an artist's eye for the beauty that exists in everyday life.

Elinor's extensive knowledge of Dublin brought her to many locations across the city. She witnessed citizens as they worked, played, shopped and prayed. Her realisation that much of what she saw was soon to disappear also added a greater poignancy to her work. The pattern-day on the outskirts of the city and the Corpus Christi procession are but two of the events which no longer form part of Dublin life. She also successfully captured the physical detail of the city. Her architectural studies show the splendour of Georgian Dublin, some of it threatened at the time, as in the case of the row of houses on Lower Fitzwilliam Street. Whilst nobody bemoaned the loss of decrepit tenement buildings, the unsympathetic manner in which some of the inner city dwellers were relocated is addressed by Elinor's York Street eviction scenes. Her empathy and understanding, coupled with her technical ability, enabled her to create many lasting and powerful images which also reveal a social concern for the problems of those being photographed.

The task of selecting for exhibition and publication a limited number of images which would truly reflect the depth and variety of themes within the collection was a difficult one. However it is hoped that the subject areas in which the images have been loosely grouped will provide a pointer towards the main concerns and motifs within her work. In the choice of title, an attempt was made to capture the mood of the collection. Elinor and her husband were neighbours and friends of the poet Patrick Kavanagh and it is because of this connection that the title 'If ever you go to Dublin town' was chosen. The poem of the same name deals with the passing of time and recalls Dublin when it had a town-like atmosphere.

It was essential that the reproduction of Elinor's work should remain faithful to the high standard of her original photography. For exhibition purposes, the images were printed in a large square format mirroring the original 6cm x 6cm negatives. The decision to refrain from cropping or framing the image made full use of the negative, ensuring that the sharp detail extending to the edge of the frame was retained. This format has been replicated in this publication.

The exhibition which opened in July 1999 attracted widespread interest. This was the first time that a National Library exhibition had focussed solely upon one photographer's work. The photographs prompted many recollections and memories and people were quick to recognise neighbours and relatives. This additional feedback was recorded giving a personal and living dimension to the research on the collection. Amongst those who visited the archive were members of the Donnelly family pictured in the York Street eviction scene. Anthony Donnelly, who features as an infant in the photograph on page 67, related how his family were later moved to the suburb of Ballymun, an area which Elinor also photographed.

In interviews with Elinor Wiltshire prior to the exhibition, she graciously discussed her influences and provided a wealth of background information which forms the basis of much of the text which appears throughout this book. She explained that she always used a Rolleiflex camera which, she felt, allowed her a greater degree of control over her final images. The viewing mechanism of the Rolleiflex camera meant that the photographer looked downwards when focussing on an image and so many people did not realise that they were being photographed; hence the natural and uninhibited manner in which they are portrayed. One exception to this practice of unobtrusive observance is the series of photographs taken with the travelling families. Elinor had befriended the families, visiting them on several occasions, and she photographed them as they went about their daily routines and in their preparation for the ancient horse fair at Cahirmee, Co. Cork. The children and adults alike appear relaxed and receptive to her interest in their lives.

In interview, Elinor cited Cartier-Bresson's street photography as her greatest influence. His photography was first shown in 1933 and captures street life across

several continents. Like him, Elinor felt that a good shot was the proper combination of several factors such as form, lighting and an emotional connection with the subject. She also maintained that it was easy to anticipate an event with lots of hustle and bustle and excellent opportunities for photographs; the scenes at Heuston station and the Cumberland Street Market are examples of this.

Sadly, Reginald Wiltshire's death in 1968 led to the sale of the couple's business and brought an end to Elinor's series of Dublin photographs. Prior to her eventual move to London, Elinor visited Ethiopia where she photographed people with her usual skill and insight. These images were exhibited at The Green Studios, perhaps the only formal showing of Elinor's work before the 1999 exhibition. Photographic exhibitions were, of course, rare occurrences during this period.

Today Elinor lives in London. She actively conducts botanical research, working one day per week in the National History Museum. She has written many influential papers on topics such as biodiversity and mosses and now uses her camera to illustrate her findings in this area. However, her keen sense of what constitutes a good picture does not go to waste: it is now employed in the creation of the bright and graphic tapestries which adorn her home.

Comparisons have been made between Elinor's work and that of the well known Fr. Browne and G.A. Duncan both active during this period. However, there appears to have been little interaction between photographers and most were working independently of one another without exchange of ideas. Elinor is one of the few female photographers from this period to have received recognition in what is essentially a male-dominated field.

Overall, little has been written on Irish photography during the latter part of this century. It is hoped that this publication of Elinor Wiltshire's work will add to the understanding of the development of photography in Ireland and women's role within it, whilst also bringing the outstanding work of this remarkable woman to a wider audience.

It has been a great privilege for me to have had the opportunity of getting to know Elinor Wiltshire and her work. I am grateful to the National Library of Ireland and to the Women's History Project for selecting me for this assignment. I want also to thank Gráinne MacLochlainn, curator of the National Photographic Archive, for her invaluable advice and assistance and to thank also the other staff of the Archive and of the Women's History Project for their support and encouragement during the assignment.

ORLA FITZPATRICK

AUGUST 1999

This cheerful couple were spotted by Elinor in York Street on the same day that she photographed the little boys featured on the front cover of this book.

1954

Grand Canal scenes

This series of images follows a Córas Iompair Éireann canal barge on its journey
from Baggot Street to Portobello Bridge. In 1950 the Grand Canal Company
was amalgamated with CIE. Commercial traffic on the canal was discontinued
soon after these photographs were taken in 1959.

Barge passing through lock gate at Portobello Bridge.
1959

Couple browsing through books outside shop, Merchant's Arch, Temple Bar.
This image shows the Commercial Buildings in the distance which were
demolished to make way for the Central Bank Headquarters.

1969

Merchant's Arch, Temple Bar.
1969

Cumberland Street Scenes

For the past sixty years a market has taken place in Cumberland Street selling
second-hand goods. This series shows shoppers and sellers amongst the jumble.
The images were all taken on a Saturday in 1969.

Nuns passing demolition on Upper Dorset Street.
The spire of the Abbey Presbyterian Church, commonly called
Findlater's Church, is visible in the distance.

1964

Georgian doorway of No. 12 Usher's Island. A nearby house on Usher's Island
was the setting for 'The Dead' the final short story in James Joyce's *Dubliners*.
1966

A Georgian doorway in good repair on Merrion Square.

1966

Joggers, Phoenix Park.
1969

Couple on motorbike, Phoenix Park.
1969

This match day series shows fans and sellers outside Heuston Station on
the morning of the All-Ireland Senior Football final on 28th September, 1969.
67,828 attended the match in which Kerry beat Offaly by 3 points.

Boy selling hats on match day.
1969

Man selling hats and rosettes outside Heuston Station.
1969

Woman selling fruit beside hoardings at demolished Nelson Pillar.
1969

Elinor took many photographs of Liffey scenes stretching from Victoria Quay to George's Quay. Included in this series are Gandon's two masterpieces the Four Courts and the Custom House.

This page shows Kingsbridge (Heuston) Station which was built as the terminus and headquarters of the Great Southern and Western Railway Company in the 1840s. The station was called Kingsbridge after the nearby cast-iron bridge.

1969

O'Donovan Rossa Bridge was built in 1813 and opened in 1816.
This image shows Christ Church Cathedral which was fully in view after
the demolition of a row of houses on Wood Quay to make way for the
second phase of the Civic Offices.

1969

View of the Four Courts from Merchant's Quay. Elinor was encouraged to
record buildings of architectural significance by Desmond Guinness of the
Georgian Society.

1966

Ormond Quay urinal with *News of the World* poster.
In 1932 a number of ornate cast-iron pissoirs were imported from France.
Most of these were erected along the Liffey quays to facilitate those
attending the Eucharistic Congress held in that year.

1969

When Liberty Hall was opened in 1965 it was the first skyscraper on the Dublin skyline. The seventeen-storey tower replaced the old headquarters of the Irish Transport and General Workers' Union which dated from the 1820s. When the new building opened it included an observation terrace from which the public could view the entire city. A bomb in 1972 blew out most of the windows and afterwards access was restricted.

1966

ELINOR WILTSHIRE

The Loop Line Bridge was completed in 1891 to provide a rail connection between Westland Row (Pearse Station) and Amiens Street (Connolly Station). Although the bridge obscures the downstream view of the Custom House, its advertising hoardings became landmarks in their own right.

1966

The foundation stone for the Custom House, James Gandon's great masterpiece, was laid in 1781 and it was completed in 1791. It cost £400,000 to build. Initially there was opposition to the building from nearby residents who feared that the proximity of commerce would reduce property values.

1966

ELINOR WILTSHIRE

When the Talbot Memorial Bridge was built in 1978 it closed the
Custom House Quay permanently to sea going vessels.
Until then Guinness boats moored at the Quay.
This picture shows one of the fleet 'The Lady Gwendoline'.

1966

Kilmainham Gaol was the County Gaol for Dublin and from 1790s to 1920s
it housed Irish revolutionaries. The gaol closed in 1924 and fell into a state of
disrepair. A voluntary committee began its restoration in 1960.

Spiral Staircase in disrepair, Kilmainham Gaol.

1953

ELINOR WILTSHIRE

Main hall and landings, East Wing, Kilmainham Gaol.
1953

Lampstandards outside No. 17 Harcourt Street.
1966

Elaborate railings, Baggot Street.
1969

Sandymount Strand which is situated just outside Dublin was a popular
destination for day-trippers, as the crowded beach demonstrates.
1969

ELINOR WILTSHIRE

Pattern Day, St. Columcille's Well, Ballycullen, Rathfarnham, Co. Dublin.

Occasions like this were commonplace throughout the country, on a saint's feastday a crowd would gather to celebrate mass and take holy water from the well. Patrick Kavanagh encouraged Elinor to record events like this which were dying out.

June 13th, 1954

Patrick Kavanagh in Ballinaclash, Co. Wicklow.
1951

To commemorate the 50th Anniversary of Bloomsday on 16th June, 1954 a group from
the Dublin literary scene retraced some of the route taken in James Joyce's *Ulysses*.
Present on this occasion were Patrick Kavanagh, John Ryan, Anthony Cronin, Brian O'Nolan
(Flann O'Brien) and Michael Scott amongst others. The group left from architect Michael Scott's
home in Sandycove, stopped off at Ringsend and finished at The Bailey public house in Duke Street.
This outing is described in John Ryan's memoir *Remembering How we Stood*.

View of horse drawn carriages outside Michael Scott's house, Sandycove, Co. Dublin.

Anthony Cronin, John Ryan and Patrick Kavanagh at Martello tower,
Bloomsday, Sandycove, Co. Dublin.

This photograph is part of the series covering the 50th anniversary of
Bloomsday, June 16th, 1954. When the group stopped in Smith's public house,
Ringsend, Elinor noticed these children playing outside a grocer's shop.

Patrick Kavanagh and Anthony Cronin seated on horse and carriage outside
Davy Byrne's pub, Bloomsday, Duke Street.

Patrick Kavanagh was born in Inniskeen, Co. Monaghan in October 1904. The poet was friendly with Elinor and her husband and suggested this visit to his birthplace. These photographs show the family farm where Kavanagh lived for thirty five years and the fields which inspired much of his poetry.

1963

Number 7 Eccles Street was the fictional home of Leopold and Molly Bloom,
characters in James Joyce's *Ulysses*. The site is now occupied by the Mater
Private Hospital.

1965

Hardwicke Street and Place were laid out between 1805–07 and formed
part of an architectural set-piece looking onto St. George's Church.
The original houses were demolished by the Corporation for new flats in 1954.

1964

Demolition work beside Kavanagh's hair studio on Charlotte Street.
Practically nothing remains of this street which was situated between
Camden Street and Harcourt Road.

1964

This row of partially demolished houses on Fitzwilliam Street Lower, formed part of a Georgian streetscape which extended from Holles Street to Lower Leeson Street. The ESB owned these properties upon which they wished to build their headquarters. Planning permission was given in 1964 and the houses were demolished in May 1965.

1965

Fitzwilliam Street Lower.
1965

Scenes like this were commonplace in Dublin, as demolitions left gaping holes
in streets and the remaining houses required support.

1964

Corpus Christi is a major feastday in the Catholic calendar and was celebrated throughout
the country with processions, altars and masses. This series of images shows a procession in
the Halston Street area of Dublin. The procession followed a route which brought it through
the grounds of the King's Inns in Henrietta Street. Young girls in their communion dresses
joined with church groups carrying banners. Streets were decorated with altars and bunting.

1969

Corpus Christi, Henrietta Street.
1969

Corpus Christi, Church Street area.
1969

Corpus Christi, Church Street area.
1969

Young woman reading newspaper beside ornate ironwork bollards,
Parnell Monument, O'Connell Street.

1969

View of Leinster Lawn through railings showing the obelisk designed by
Raymond MacGrath. This monument commemorates the deaths of
Arthur Griffith, Michael Collins and Kevin O'Higgins. It replaced an earlier
Celtic cross structure known as The Cenotaph.

1966

These images show fine examples of the ornate ironwork found in much of Dublin's street furniture. Elinor believed that these details contributed to the overall look and atmosphere in the city.

Lamppost depicting 'sea-horses' on Grattan Bridge.
1966

Harcourt Street bootscraper.
1969

Railing detail, Earlsfort Terrace.
1969

Detail of ornate leaf ironwork, Clyde Road, Ballsbridge.

1964

A glasshouse in the Botanic Gardens, Glasnevin, Dublin.
1969

Children skipping in front of Ballymun tower blocks which were designed by English architect Arthur Swift and completed in 1967. The high rise was heralded as an answer to housing problems however the scheme received much criticism for its anti-social layout. It is due for demolition in the near future.

1969

The War Memorial Gardens at Islandbridge are dedicated to the memory of the
49,400 Irish soldiers who died in the 1914–1918 war. The names of all the soldiers
are contained in the granite bookrooms in the gardens which were designed by
Sir Edwin Lutyens.

1969

Pram in doorway, Townsend Street.
1969

This image shows families protesting against evictions in York Street.
The Georgian houses in the background illustrate the deterioration
that was typical in many tenements.

1964

This cluttered shop window near Winetavern Street is typical of the area.
It shows an assortment of second hand and new goods. The area was occupied
by generations of 'clothes brokers'. This row was demolished in 1964.
1953

Shoppers on Michael's Hill, Winetavern Street.
1953

The Irish House on Wood Quay at the corner of Winetavern Street was built in 1870. The façade was decorated with Celtic revival and nationalist subjects by stuccodores Burnet and Comerford. It was demolished in the mid 1960s to make way for the Civic Offices. The plaster figures were transferred to the Guinness Museum.

1964

Aerial view of Dublin from the tower of St. Audoen's Church of Ireland,
Cornmarket showing the Four Courts in the distance. St Audoen's
is the only medieval church in the city.

1968

The Five Lamps is a Dublin landmark erected in memory of Galwegian,
General Henry Hall who served with the British Army in India.
The image shows workers cycling home at evening time.

1964

The Nelson Pillar was erected in memory of Admiral Nelson and afforded Dubliners a magnificent view of their city. On the night of 7th March, 1966 the upper half of the column was shattered by an explosion. This image was taken early on the following morning. The remainder was blown up by army engineers.

Elinor recorded travellers in preparation for the Cahirmee horse fair, Buttevant, Co. Cork.
The one day horse fair was attended by many travellers who adorned their traditional style
caravans with paper flowers. She also visited families at a campsite in Loughrea, Co. Galway
where she photographed everyday scenes of work and play.

Two little boys at the Sheridan/O'Brien campsite, Loughrea, Co. Galway.
1954

Traveller couple, Buttevant, Co. Cork.
1954

Woman washing clothes at Sheridan/O'Brien campsite, Loughrea, Co. Galway.
1954

Blacksmith at Sheridan/O'Brien campsite, Loughrea, Co. Galway.
1954

Detail of caravan wheel, Buttevant, Co. Cork.
1954

Women and children at decorated caravan, Buttevant, Co. Cork.
1954

PAGE	TITLE	CODE
Cover	Two little boys, York Street	WIL e2[54]
1	Couple at window, York Street	WIL e3[54]
2	Man looking out of barge, Grand Canal	WIL j2[59]
3	Leafy bank, Grand Canal	WIL i4[59]
4	Barge passing through lock, Grand Canal	WIL j12[59]
5	Boy at Portobello, Grand Canal	WIL j11[59]
6	Couple at shop, Merchant's Arch	WIL57[7]
7	Child running past shops, Merchant's Arch	WIL57[9]
8	Children in car, Cumberland Street	WIL55[6]
9	Children with suitcase, Cumberland Street	WIL42[10]
10	Boy in party hat, Cumberland Street	WIL56[6]
11	Book browser, Cumberland Street	WIL55[8]
12	Boy near holy picture, Cumberland Street	WIL56[8]
13	Nuns passing demolition, Dorset Street	WIL10[1]
14	Georgian doorway, Usher's Island	WIL19[12]
15	Georgian doorway, Merrion Square	WIL24[6]
16	Joggers, Phoenix park	WIL54[10]
17	Motorcyclists, Phoenix park	WIL54[9]
18	Crowd arriving for match, Heuston Station	WIL58[2]
19	Boy selling hats, Heuston Station	WIL58[1]
20	Man selling badges, Heuston Station	WIL58[5]
21	Fruit seller, Heuston Station	WIL58[10]
22	Heuston Station and bridge	WIL44[7]
23	Christ Church Cathedral and Wood Quay	WIL65[2]
24	The Four Courts and the river Liffey	WIL27[1]
25	Urinal on Ormond Quay	WIL41[12]
26	Liberty Hall	WIL23[5]
27	Loopline Bridge with Rowntrees Sign	WIL31[7]
28	The Customs House	WIL23[6]
29	Man walking on George's Quay	WIL23[2]
30	Spiral staircase, Kilmainham Gaol	WIL b2[53]
31	Main hall, Kilmainham Gaol	WIL d5[53]
32	Lampstandards, Harcourt Street	WIL22[10]
33	Railings, Baggot Street	WIL61[6]
34	Girl walking on wall, Sandymount Strand	WIL48[1]
35	Two girls playing, Sandymount Strand	WIL44[6]
36	Young girl and man, Ballycullen	WIL f3[54]
37	Two men in conversation, Ballycullen	WIL f8[54]
38	Woman and children praying, Ballycullen	WIL f2[54]
39	Patrick Kavanagh, Ballinaclash, Wicklow	WIL pk10[4]
40	Aerial view of Michael Scott's house, Sandycove	WIL pk11[8]
41	Anthony Cronin, John Ryan and Patrick Kavanagh	WIL pk11[9]
42	Ringsend Shop front	WIL pk12[8]

ACKNOWLEDGEMENTS

The Women's History Association of Ireland undertook the organisation of the Women's History Project in September 1997. We would like to record our thanks to the WHAI and to the committee of the Women's History Project. Funding provided by the Department of Arts, Heritage, Gaeltacht and the Islands made the Women's History Project possible. We would like to thank the Minister, Síle de Valera TD, for her support. Special thanks must also go to Brigid MacManus, Conor O'Malley, and Joe Meleady of the department. The Women's History Project has received much support from the Irish Manuscripts Commission, particularly from Professor Geoffrey Hand, chairman of the Commission, and Professors Mary Daly and Declan Kiberd. Margaret Clancy, secretary to the Commission, has provided assistance in a number of ways and we are grateful to her for that. We are very grateful to the Heritage Council for funding, through the Women's History Project, the cataloguing of the Wiltshire Collection.

The staff in the National Photographic Archive have contributed in various ways towards the compilation of this publication and are acknowledged with thanks, Angela Kelly, Siobhan O'Rourke, Dave McLoughlin, John Browne, Martin Horan, Karen Dignan and Sandra Conroy. John Farrell and Eugene Hogan, the Library's photographer, have also assisted with the exhibition. We are also grateful to Mary Doherty and the staff of Red Dog, Andrè Gardner of GMS and the staff of Woodprint Finishing who all contributed to the popular exhibition. Thanks are also due to Theresa O'Donnell, Archivist at Guinness Ireland Group and the staff of the following institutions: Pavee Point, Kilmainham Gaol the Phoenix Park Visitor Centre and the Patrick Kavanagh Centre who provided information utilised within the text. Ann Egan (ex-The Green Studio) kindly provided background information on the type of work undertaken by the studio. Thanks are also due to Professor Declan Kiberd whose address provided insight and entertainment on the opening night of the exhibition.